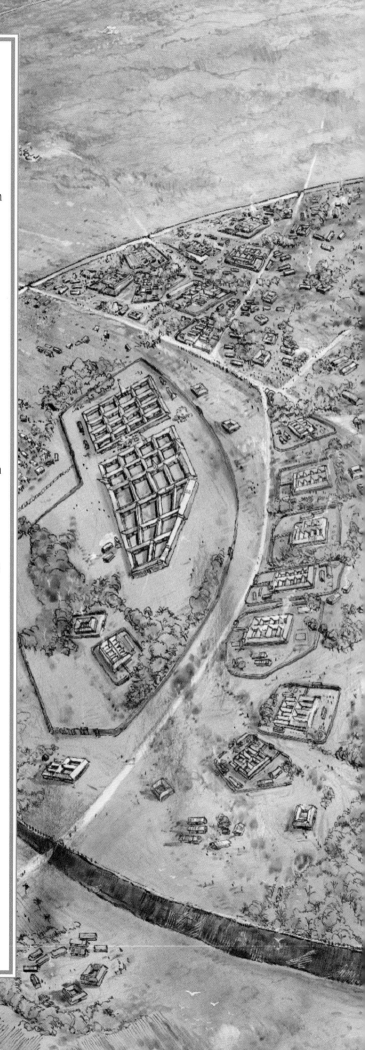

Editor: Penny Clarke
Consultants: Charles Gore
　　　　　　　Obi Patience Igwara

FIONA MACDONALD

studied history at Cambridge University and the University of East Anglia. She has taught in schools and adult education and written many children's books on historical subjects, including *How Would You Survive in Aztec Times?* and *Keeping Clean, A Very Peculiar History*, which won the Times Educational Supplement's Information Book award for 1995.

CHARLES GORE

studied anthropology at Cambridge University, later specializing in African Studies at the School of Oriental and African Studies, University of London. Since 1986 he has done much fieldwork in Benin City and written on the art and culture of West Africa.

OBI PATIENCE IGWARA

was educated in Nigeria and the London School of Economics. She has lectured on sociology at the universities of Warwick and Leeds and is now Kirk-Greene Junior Research Fellow at Oxford. She is a founder-member of the Association for the Study of Ethnicity and Nationalism.

GERALD WOOD

was born in London and began his career in film advertising. He then illustrated magazines for many years before becoming a book illustrator specializing in historical reconstruction.

DAVID SALARIYA

studied illustration and printmaking in Dundee, Scotland. He has created many books for publishers in the UK and overseas, including the award-winning *Very Peculiar History* series. In 1989 he set up The Salariya Book Company. He lives in Brighton with his wife, the illustrator Shirley Willis, and their son Jonathan.

Produced by
The SALARIYA BOOK CO. LTD
25 Marlborough Place
Brighton BN1 1UB

Published in 1998 by
Franklin Watts
96 Leonard Street
London EC2A 4RH

First American edition 1998 by
Franklin Watts
A Division of Grolier Publishing
Sherman Turnpike
Danbury, CT 06816

ISBN 0-531-14481-X

A copy of the Cataloging-in-publication data is available from the Library of Congress

METROPOLIS

ANCIENT AFRICAN TOWN

Written by Fiona Macdonald
Illustrated by Gerald Wood

Created and designed by David Salariya

W
FRANKLIN WATTS
A Division of Grolier Publishing
NEW YORK • LONDON • HONG KONG • SYDNEY
DANBURY, CONNECTICUT

CONTENTS

INTRODUCTION

This book is a tour of a West African town in the late 17th century. The town is based on the great city of Benin, but because descriptions of Benin vary, no one now can be absolutely sure of its layout.

Benin City was the capital of the Edo empire, which was also known as the empire of Benin. Its boundaries changed from time to time, according to the strength and military success of different rulers. At its largest it covered an area stretching from the Lagos lagoon in the west to the River Niger in the east. The people who lived around Benin City called themselves the "Edo." They spoke a language known as Edo, which is still spoken by millions of people in Nigeria. And Benin City itself still exists. It, too, is in present-day Nigeria.

According to African tradition, the Edo became powerful between 1200 and 1300. They expanded their city, started new farms and villages, and built huge earthworks to mark their boundaries. They were renowned in Africa as warriors, traders, and metalworkers. Between 1472 and 1486 the first Portuguese explorers arrived in Benin. From then until the end of the 19th century, Benin's rulers and merchants became wealthy through international trade.

Benin was ruled by sacred kings called Obas. Everyone else, however wealthy, had to obey the Oba. The name of the first family of Obas meant "lord of the sky," which shows how powerful they were. Palace Chiefs and Town Chiefs helped the Obas rule their empire.

AROUND THE TOWN

Queen Mother's Palace
Now you are outside the city, but there are still some splendid buildings to see. This is the palace where the Queen Mother lives. You can find out about her royal duties on pages 32 and 33.

Oba's Shrine
On pages 14 and 15 you can find out more about this holy shrine. You can also discover why ancestors were important to the people of Benin.

Oba's Market
What will you buy from this market? There are goods from Benin and far beyond its borders. Make your choice on pages 20 and 21.

Oba's Palace
Who lives in this splendid building? Why is there a snake on the roof? Find out on pages 12 and 13.

Storytellers' Corner
Sit down, relax, and enjoy a story. You might learn something of Benin's history, too. You can read one ancient, but very popular, tale on pages 22 and 23.

Brassworkers' Ward
The beautiful, intricate brass statues produced in Benin are famous far beyond the empire's borders. But however are they made? You'll find the answer on pages 26 and 27.

Clothes and Weavers
The clothes of the people you'll see are wonderfully colorful. Weaving cloth is very skilled work. Learn more on pages 28 and 29.

Metalworkers' Ward
Benin is famous for the work of its craftsmen. On pages 18 and 19 you can learn more about their work.

Walls and Gates
You cannot visit Benin City without passing through these gates. The guards on duty will want to know why you are visiting the city. Tell them on pages 30 and 31.

Villages and Farms
These villagers grow food for all the citizens to eat. On pages 34 and 35 you can learn about how they farm and the crops they grow.

Chiefs' Quarters
This is where the Town Chiefs live. Who are they and what do they do? Learn about their busy and important lives on pages 24 and 25.

Great Procession
Who is this, riding so proudly through the streets? Why are there leopards in the procession? Turn to pages 16 and 17 to discover the answers.

THE OBA'S PALACE

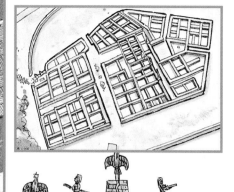

Visitors to Benin City are always impressed by the royal palace. It is very large and symbolizes the Oba's wealth and power. It has separate areas for the palace officials and the Oba's wives and children, as well as special chambers for the Oba himself. There are also guardrooms, stores for food and weapons, and many shrines.

The Oba's palace is the finest and most important building in Benin City. Its walls are decorated with ribbed mud plaster and designs of spirits and mythical creatures. The palace's rooms are grouped around courtyards and decorated with elaborate bronze plaques and wood-carvings.

Music is important in royal ceremonies. Drummers stand or sit cross-legged to play their hollow wooden drums.

As a sign of hospitality, the Oba's visitors are offered kola nuts from fine bronze containers like this fish.

The Oba's palace has a massive entrance gateway. The tall tower is decorated with a huge brass snake – a sign of royal power. On the roof are statues of birds and soldiers.

Visiting the royal palace is an important event even for powerful chiefs and successful warriors. Everyone wears their best clothes as a sign of respect for the Oba. These men are wearing necklaces of coral and cloth kilts and are carrying swords and spears. The small figures are their servants. One blows a trumpet, the other carries a box of treasure.

One of the plaques decorating the Oba's palace shows two men holding swords beside a chief. They believe the bells they wear will give them protection in battle.

THE OBA'S SHRINE

F ew visitors see the holiest part of the palace where the Oba has the shrines of his ancestors. Most families have shrines to honor their ancestors and ask for their help. Because the Oba is almost a god, his shrines are special and are believed to help the whole empire. Statues or bronze portrait heads stand on the mud altars, while elephant tusks, wooden staffs, and brass bells (to summon good spirits and scare away bad ones) are placed close by. "Thunder-stones" (prehistoric stone axes) represent the Oba's magic powers. Each dead Oba has a shrine in the palace.

Ofoe, the spirit called the Messenger of Death (below), is the servant of Ogiuwu, ruler of the kingdom of the dead. Ofoe is always shown as a head with arms and legs. He symbolizes the Oba's power of life and death over his people. If the Oba sends a little statue of Ofoe to wrongdoers, it is a warning that they will be put to death if they do not behave.

An Oba sits on his throne surrounded by servants and body-guards. This statue is on his altar in the palace as a reminder that he must still be respected.

Oba Ohen is shown with legs like mudfish, symbols of the sea god, Olokun. One tradition claims that Ohen's legs became paralyzed and he was killed when this was discovered.

The people of Benin believe a person's spirit lives in their head. So they make statues of their dead ancestors' heads to preserve their memory and keep close to their spirits.

THE GREAT PROCESSION

Ceremonial processions are important in Benin. They are part of the traditional religious festivals that are celebrated throughout the year. Each festival has a special purpose. Some are connected with farming and celebrate the clearing of new land or a good yam harvest. Others are designed to purify and strengthen the empire and keep the Oba powerful. Some festivals are secret. They take place inside the palace, and only the Oba and a few honored chiefs take part. Other festivals are public. There is singing and dancing in the streets, and the Oba, in his ceremonial robes and headdress, goes in procession around the palace walls. He is accompanied by his chiefs and high-ranking soldiers, with musicians and court entertainers following behind.

Horses are very rare in Benin because the climate is much too hot for them. Sometimes an Oba keeps one or two as status symbols.

When the Oba and his chiefs dance at festivals, they carry ceremonial swords (above).

Leopards are a sign of royal power in Benin. The Oba keeps some in his palace. They are tamed – some say by magic charms – and trained to take part in the processions at religious festivals.

METALWORKERS' WARD

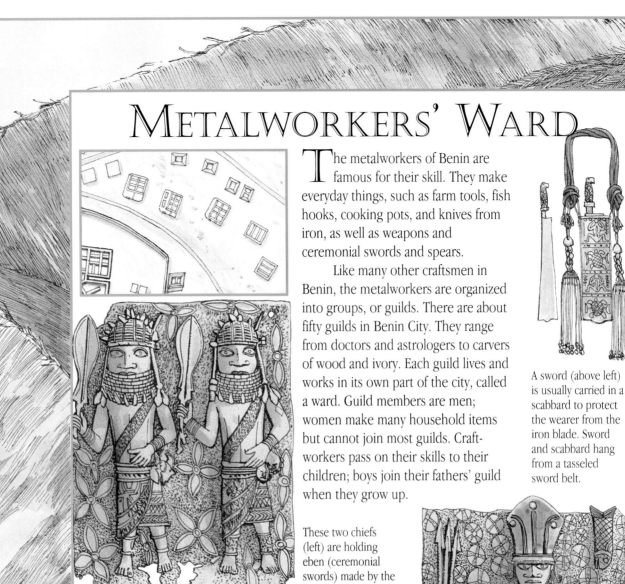

The metalworkers of Benin are famous for their skill. They make everyday things, such as farm tools, fish hooks, cooking pots, and knives from iron, as well as weapons and ceremonial swords and spears.

Like many other craftsmen in Benin, the metalworkers are organized into groups, or guilds. There are about fifty guilds in Benin City. They range from doctors and astrologers to carvers of wood and ivory. Each guild lives and works in its own part of the city, called a ward. Guild members are men; women make many household items but cannot join most guilds. Craft-workers pass on their skills to their children; boys join their fathers' guild when they grow up.

A sword (above left) is usually carried in a scabbard to protect the wearer from the iron blade. Sword and scabbard hang from a tasseled sword belt.

These two chiefs (left) are holding eben (ceremonial swords) made by the city's metalworkers.

Armed for battle, the chief (right) holds a shield in one hand and three arrows in the other. The metal arrowtips are often dipped in poison made from forest plants.

Long iron spears (left) are important weapons because soldiers do not have to get as close to their enemies as they do if they use swords. Benin's soldiers carry shields made from raffia, a stringy plant fiber.

THE OBA'S MARKET

There are several markets in Benin City and the surrounding countryside, but this is the biggest. It belongs to the Oba and is close to his palace. Most of the traders are women; some sell goods made by their families, such as leather belts and tunics or wooden cups and bowls. Others sell animals caught by hunters in the rain forest, such as monkeys, parrots, or cane rats. There are also mudfish from the river and chickens and vegetables from farms.

The richest market traders sell expensive imported goods. Brass, cloth, and glass beads come from Italy and the Netherlands. Fine striped cloth is imported by European traders or comes from other African kingdoms.

Decorated leather fan (right). The Oba gives fans like this to his chiefs.

Two views of the figures carved on a coconut drinking flask (above). It hangs from a metal chain.

Benin's carvers are famous for their skill. Below is the seat of an elaborately carved wooden stool.

A magnificent pottery bowl (above). Bowls like this are among a family's most prized possessions. They are placed on the family's shrine in honor of the god Olokun. The python modeled writhing around the bowl is one of Olokun's symbols.

STORYTELLERS' CORNER

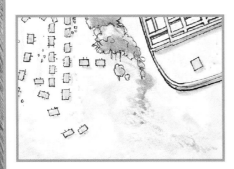

Storytelling plays an important part in the lives of the people of Benin. There are often storytellers in a shady part of the market. They usually attract a good crowd of laughing, chattering children and anyone else with time to spare. However, most storytelling is done at home in the evening, after the day's work is over.

Storytellers, whether at home or in the market, enthrall their audience with jokes and songs and many amazing tales. But storytelling is much more than just entertainment. The people of Benin do not have a written language, so by remembering and retelling ancient legends and myths, the storytellers are the historians and journalists of Benin. Instead of recording information by writing it down, they memorize it, passing it on from one generation to the next for hundreds of years. Like journalists, they also comment on current affairs by adding up-to-date details or jokes about famous people each time they retell one of the ancient tales.

THE STORY OF OGUN AND EMOTAN

The people of Benin have many stories about their ancestors and their history. One of the most popular stories is about Prince Ogun. His elder brother was the Oba, and Ogun was the heir to the throne. But the Oba's chiefs were jealous of Ogun. They told the Oba that Ogun was plotting to overthrow him and take the throne. Ogun was banished to the rain forest.

After many years in the rain forest, Ogun decided it was time to return to Benin. He had heard that his brother was a cruel ruler.

Ogun had a cousin, Emotan. She was old and childless and worked in the Oba's market. She was well known for her kindness.

Ogun went to visit Emotan secretly, but she gave him bad news: Some of the chiefs would not like him to return to Benin.

It was true. One of the chiefs, Ogiefa, seemed sympathetic, but when the two met, Ogiefa took Ogun prisoner and threw him in a well.

After being freed by Ogiefa's chief slave, Ogun went to see Emotan. Together they planned to overthrow the Oba as he visited the market.

Hiding in the crowd thronging around the Oba's procession, Ogun then confronted his brother and killed him with a spear.

The people of Benin greeted the news of the cruel Oba's death with joy, and Ogun was crowned as Oba Ewuare. He became a very great Oba.

But the new Oba's joy was short-lived. His cousin Emotan, who had given him so much help in overthrowing the tyrant, died.

Ewuare had a tree planted where her market stall had been and ordered every procession to pause there as a mark of respect.

In the 1950s a statue replaced the tree, but processions still stop there and make offerings in memory of Emotan, who helped her people.

CHIEFS' QUARTERS

The Oba is the most powerful person in Benin. The lives and deaths of all his subjects are in his hands. But two groups of important men also wield great power – the Palace Chiefs and the Town Chiefs.

Palace Chiefs are members of ancient city families. Most have noble titles. They run the Oba's palace, organize religious ceremonies, and advise the royal family. They live close to the Oba's palace.

Town Chiefs are different. They come from quite ordinary families and have earned riches and respect through their own efforts. They may have been very brave in battle, become rich through hard work as traders, or been famous for their skill as craftsmen. The Oba often appoints them to look after the interests of outlying villages. Town Chiefs also collect taxes and tribute, conscript soldiers to serve in the army, and enforce royal orders. They live in fine houses in their own quarter of Benin City, separated from the Oba's palace by the wide main road.

The house of a Town Chief (below). It is built of mud reinforced with wood. It is laid out around two big covered courtyards. Open-sided living rooms, stores, altars, and hearths are arranged around each courtyard.

All the buildings have thick thatch roofs to stop the heavy tropical rain from getting in. The thatch is made from the stringy fibers of raffia supported on a framework of wooden poles. The roofs have a shallow slope, over-hanging and protecting the buildings' thick mud walls. Rain running off the roofs of houses is stored and used for cooking and drinking.

You'll know which houses belong to the Town and Palace Chiefs by the outside walls (below). The walls of homes belonging to ordinary people are quite plain. In contrast, the homes of the Chiefs, like the walls of the Oba's palace, have wonderful decorations molded into the mud, ranging from a plain "ribbed" effect to patterns of mythical beasts and spirits.

The buildings in Benin are made of mud. First a deep pit is dug to find and extract red clay.

Big clods of clay are broken up. Then the builders jump into the pit and trample on the clay.

Building begins when the clay is a sticky mud. If rain is likely, the clay pit is covered with leaves.

The builders make wide layers of hard-packed mud about 20 inches (50 centimeters) high, leave them to harden, and then add the next layer.

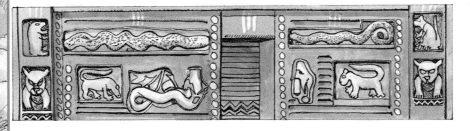

BRASSWORKERS' WARD

THE LOST-WAX METHOD OF CASTING

The most skillful of Benin's metal-workers are those who make the statues and plaques from bronze (a mixture of copper and tin) or brass (copper and zinc). Both metals are prized because they do not rust or rot in Benin's hot, humid climate. Metal plaques and statues are made by the "lost-wax" method of casting. Cheaper brass and bronze objects are made by hammering sheets of metal into different shapes.

Benin has no deposits of copper, so the raw materials for brass and bronze are imported. Benin merchants exchange ivory, pepper, and slaves with Dutch and Portuguese traders for "manillas," heavy bracelets made of leaded brass (brass mixed with lead). These are easy to melt down and use to make works of art.

Craftsmen in metal and wood decorate their work with abstract designs and patterns. These are inspired by the plants and animals around them.

A craftsman makes a solid clay core for the sculpture that will be cast in bronze or brass. It stands on a firm clay base.

When the clay core is dry and hard, it is coated in layers of wax made by the wild bees that live in the rain forest.

The craftsman carves the detail of the final statue, such as the head-dress and jewelry, in the wax.

The wax is covered with a thin slip (layer) of fine clay and left to dry. Then another layer is put on top.

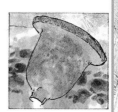

This layer of clay is also allowed to dry. The process is repeated as more layers of clay are added.

A "runner" hole is made through the clay at the top. This is so the wax can run out when the mold is heated.

Then the mold is put in a furnace full of burning wood. As the clay mold gets hot, the wax inside melts and runs out.

When all the wax has run out, the mold is put in a pit of hot ashes. This keeps the mold from cracking.

Then molten metal is poured into the mold through the hole, filling the gap where the wax had been.

When the metal is cold and hard, the mold is taken from the pit of ashes, and the clay is carefully chipped away.

When all the clay has been removed, the craftsman adds the finest details to the statue. Finally, he polishes it.

All Benin's best statues are made like this – it is called the "lost-wax" method because the wax is lost.

CLOTHES AND WEAVERS

The people of Benin wear bright and colorful clothes woven from many different kinds of fiber: wool, cotton, raffia, and bast (the fiber of another kind of plant). The weavers have guilds, just like the other crafts. The men who weave the cloth for the Oba's clothes belong to a special, separate guild.

As usual, women are not allowed to belong to the weavers' guilds. Women do weave, but in their own homes where they make cloth for their family's needs. However, in the palace, there is a special group of women who weave elaborate wigs from animal hair for the important chiefs to wear on ceremonial occasions.

At festivals the chiefs wear bronze pendants like these, which hang from belts around their waists.

Men wear kilts to below the knee, often decorated with elaborate patterns. Older women wear longer wrap-around dresses in similar fabrics. Chiefs are distinguished by their long robes and the fine coral jewelry they wear around their necks and wrists.

Weavers produce long strips of cloth about 6 in (16 cm) wide on their looms. Clothes are then made by sewing several of these strips together. As well as weaving cloth for clothes, weavers also make the cloth from which sword scabbards and waist pendants are made.

Chiefs also wear colorful woven waist pendants (right). When they are not wearing the pendants, the chiefs hang them on the walls of their family shrine.

Dyes for the cloth are made from plants and crushed earth. Some are made locally; others are imported from Europe. Certain colors have religious meanings. White, the color of purity, belongs to Olokun, the great sea god. Black belongs to Ogiuwu, god of death, and red is the color of Ogun, god of hunters, craftsmen, farmers, and warriors.

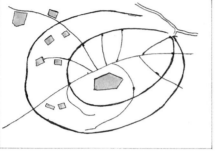

The Oba of Benin is strong and feared by many neighboring rulers. At short notice he can mobilize up to 20,000 soldiers. But the Oba also has many bitter enemies, and the empire has been invaded many times. So, to protect himself and his subjects from sudden attack, the city is surrounded with massive earth walls. Around the outside of the walls is a deep ditch from which the earth for the walls was dug.

Anyone entering or leaving the city of Benin has to pass through one of the nine great gates in the city wall. These are made of the toughest rain forest timber and are very strong. Each one is under constant guard by a chief and his troops, who will probably challenge you as you enter the city. Be polite and respectful and you won't have any trouble. It is reported that when Oba Ewuare rebuilt the walls (in the 15th century AD), he gave the gates extra protection by burying a magic charm under each one.

Plan of the city walls (top) made in the 17th century by one of the first Europeans to visit Benin. The present walls have been built up over many years and are 7 miles (11.5 km) in circumference. It is almost 56 feet (17 m) from the top of the walls to the bottom of the ditch.

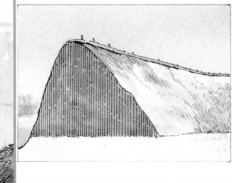

There are also large earthworks outside the city. Some of these are for defense; others mark the boundaries between land belonging to different communities. All together, the walls are 9,900 mi (16,000 km) long and cover an area of over 2,500 sq mi (6,500 sq km).

The walls in and around Benin City are the second largest man-made structure after the Great Wall of China.

QUEEN MOTHER'S PALACE

The Oba has many wives – usually over a hundred. He marries most of them for political reasons, often to make peace with neighboring kings.

The Oba's wives and children live in a special part of the royal palace. The Oba's mother, however, does not live in the palace, so she cannot interfere. In fact, by law, the Oba and his mother must not see each other. So the Queen Mother has a fine palace outside the city walls. She is honored like a senior chief, rules over all the farms and villages near her palace, and appoints her own chiefs.

A statuette showing a Queen Mother and her attendants, two of whom are shielding her from the sun.

Queen Idia of Benin (above), whose son Oba Esigie ruled in the 15th century, is honored for the part she played in helping to defeat the Attah of Idah, who ruled a kingdom north of Benin.

Each Queen Mother has a shrine in her honor in the palace.

Models like this are placed on the shrines in the Queen Mother's Palace.

VILLAGES AND FARMS

The empire of Benin varies in size according to the military successes of the different Obas, but it is one of the largest West African kingdoms. Much of it is dense tropical rain forest, but there are also many farms, villages, and towns. Most people make their living from farming, or from hunting animals and birds and catching fish.

Yams are the most important crop. The farmers clear the ground in February, cutting down and burning the vegetation. In April they plant seed-yams. The crop of new yams will be ready to harvest between September and November. Farmers also grow pepper, coffee, bitter leaf, and okra. They gather kola nuts and fruits, like papaya, from the forest. From palm trees they collect fruit, sap to make palm-wine, and oil for cooking. Pepper is grown both to sell to foreign traders and to use in cooking.

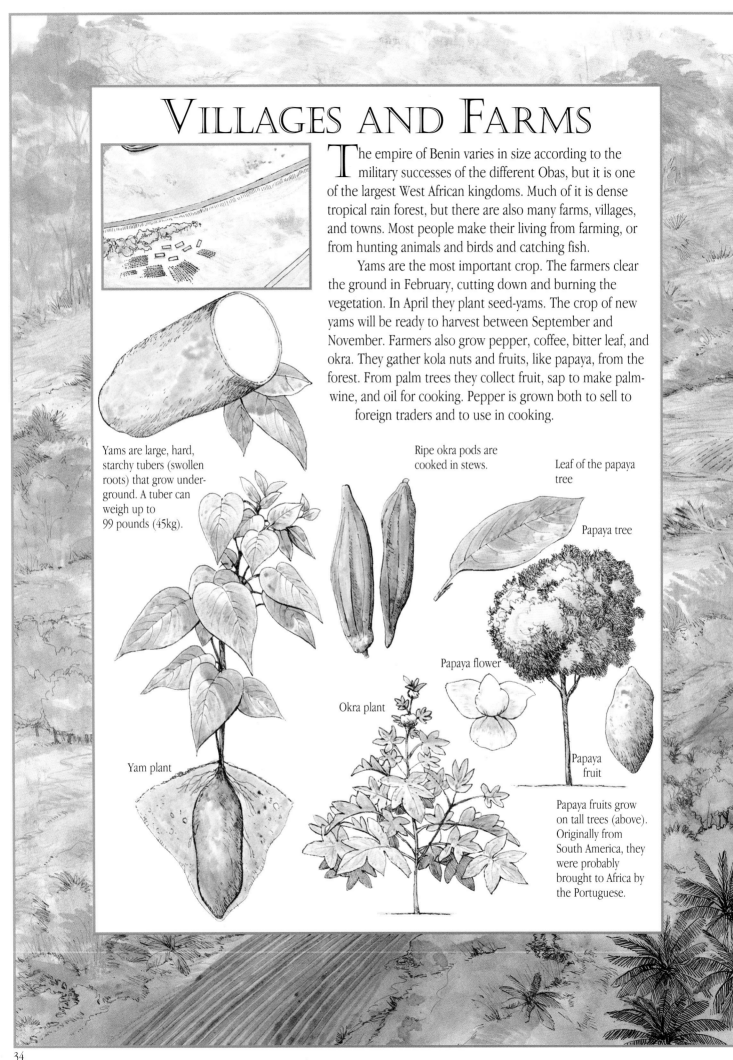

Yams are large, hard, starchy tubers (swollen roots) that grow under-ground. A tuber can weigh up to 99 pounds (45kg).

Ripe okra pods are cooked in stews.

Leaf of the papaya tree

Papaya tree

Papaya flower

Okra plant

Papaya fruit

Yam plant

Papaya fruits grow on tall trees (above). Originally from South America, they were probably brought to Africa by the Portuguese.

Time-Traveler's Guide

When to Visit

The climate of Benin is truly tropical. The temperature is hot and scarcely varies all year. During the day it averages about 86°F (30°C), while at night it seldom falls below 68°F (20°C). Rainfall is high during the rainy season, which lasts from May to November, with a brief (two-week) break in August. Over 117 in (3,000 millimeters) of rain can fall in a single year! And it is humid almost year-round.

Unless you are used to coping with monsoon rain and mud, it might be better to visit toward the end of the rainy season or at the beginning of the dry season. Then you can be sure of brilliant, hot sunshine. But be warned! Toward the end of December the wind blows from the Sahara Desert, and you can encounter great clouds of dust. Then everything is covered with a dust haze, and the dust itself cakes your legs and feet, stings your eyes, chokes your throat, and gets tangled in your hair. Some travelers find dust even more unpleasant than mud.

How to Travel

Like everyone else in Benin, you will travel on foot. The very rich or very important sometimes travel in litters carried by their servants.

On ceremonial occasions the Oba rides on a horse, with two senior chiefs walking on each side. The Oba has magnificent stables in his royal palace, but you will rarely see horses elsewhere in Benin. They do not thrive in its hot climate. And, because there are few horses, there are no carriages or farm carts. The people of Benin carry everything they need, from firewood and drinking water to fresh fruit and colorful cloth, in bowls and baskets on their heads. If they live beside the river, they may also carry heavy loads by dugout canoe.

In the countryside, muddy paths can be quite an obstacle. At the end of the dry season the rains are welcome, but they produce a great deal of sticky mud, which makes getting around very difficult, especially if you are planning to trek along country roads.

What to Eat and Drink

Yams are the staple food of Benin. You will find them cooked in several ways – fried, roasted, or stewed. But mostly they are boiled and pounded and made into small balls to be served with meat or fish stews. They taste a lot like potatoes – plain, but they are very filling and good for you. Benin people get about two-thirds of their nourishment from starchy plant foods like yams. To liven up the taste, they use pepper and eat them with stews that have mudfish, cane rat, or vegetables in them.

Rich people, like the Oba and the Palace Chiefs, eat beef, mutton, and chicken roasted or fried in palm oil with their okra or yams; ordinary people eat dried fish, bitter leaf, or beans. Cane rats caught in the forest are a succulent treat.

For your second course, try some of the many different fruits. Mangoes and papayas are the most popular.

To drink there is usually just water – although if you can afford it, you could try some palm wine.

TIME-TRAVELER'S GUIDE

WHAT TO WEAR

Benin is a tropical country and the weather is warm all year round, so you will not need to wear very many clothes. Many children and young unmarried people wear nothing at all. Take a tip from the older people – loose, elegant styles, such as kilts for men or ankle-length robes for women, are more comfortable than tightly fitting designs in the hot, humid climate. Clothes made from the fibers of plants that grow locally, such as cotton or raffia, are the most pleasant to wear.

Remember, the sun's heat is often very intense, so it is best to wear a hat or be like the Oba and use a sunshade. When-ever the Oba goes through the streets in procession, chiefs walk beside him and protect him with a huge sunshade.

Local people usually go barefoot, and you might like to copy them. The streets and houses of Benin are always very clean, so dirty feet will not be a problem – except for mud in the rainy season. However, if you do decide to walk barefoot, take care not to step on snakes or scorpions!

WHAT TO BUY

The markets in Benin are full of many wonderful goods to buy. The people of Benin are great traders, and the markets sell goods from all Benin's neighboring states in West Africa. There are fantastic fabrics – lengths of brightly striped cloth and deep blue cotton — pepper, stone beads, and semiprecious stones of red and yellow agate.

You might also like to buy some of the fine white cotton cloth that wealthy local people wear as flowing robes. Or else there are iron and copper rings, bracelets, and anklets, but you may find these rather heavy if you intend to do much sight-seeing.

If you have time – and the right sort of hair – you might like to pay a visit to a hairdresser. Women in Benin pride themselves on having beautiful hairstyles, with elaborate braids and curls. Some women also like to treat their hair with roasted palm-nut oil. This oil gives the hair a wonderful sheen, which is extremely fashionable at the moment.

HOW TO PAY

Traders in Benin do not use coins. They either barter goods – that is, they exchange what they have to sell for other goods of about the same value – or use cowrie shells or manillas (Portuguese brass bracelets) in place of coins. Many popular goods for barter come from Europe – for example, red velvet, Venetian crystal beads, gilded mirrors, and red glass earrings. You might like to bring some with you if you intend to buy a lot of things. But don't worry if you didn't think of doing this; just stock up on cowrie shells before you go to the market. If you are a seasoned traveler you may already have some – they come from the Indian Ocean and are traded by merchants from East Africa. Otherwise merchants in the main market-place will give you cowries in exchange for some of your gold coins.

Alternatively, if you plan to stop at a Portuguese or Dutch port on your way to Africa, you can get a supply of manillas, which traders in Benin will accept as currency.

GOVERNMENT FIGURES

The Oba has many people to help him rule: the most important are the Uzama (hereditary chiefs), the Town Chiefs, and the Palace Chiefs.

The Uzama rule over the farms and villages on the outskirts of Benin City. The Oba's first son and heir is one of these hereditary chiefs.

The Town Chiefs are appointed by the Oba from among the strongest and most successful people in the empire. They act as a council and give the Oba advice. The Iyase is the principal Town Chief, and it is his duty to act as a counterbalance to the Oba, to prevent him from becoming too powerful.

The Palace Chiefs head the three Palace Associations. These associations are traditional religious and ceremonial groups, and everybody in Benin belongs to one. Some of the Palace Chiefs have mostly religious duties. Others organize the running of the palace and arrange meetings between the Oba and important people from outside. A third group guards the Oba's many wives and children.

LAW & ORDER

In Benin City, each guild maintains law and order in its own part of the city. In the villages it is groups of elders who keep law and order and watch out for bad behavior. They also organize the village's younger age groups.

The people of Benin are famous for their friendliness and good manners to each other and to visitors – they consider these qualities the marks of an honorable man. So, if you get lost while exploring the city, you'll find people very helpful.

There are strict laws against theft and cheating. A Benin citizen who steals from a foreigner can be put to death. A traveler who steals is unlikely to be executed but will almost certainly be swiftly expelled from the country.

While you are exploring, keep an eye open for important-looking people carrying white sticks. These are palace officials on business for the Oba; it is a serious offense to get in their way. They are probably taking presents of kola nuts and spices to favored merchants or senior chiefs.

BENIN SOCIETY

Benin society is organized into several different groups – based on family, jobs, skills, age, and wealth. An individual can belong to several groups at once – for example, a family group, an age group, and a group of workers doing the same job. As a general rule, people who are old, rich, and experienced are the most powerful and the most highly respected.

Servant-slaves are at the other end of the scale in Benin society. They are legally bound to work for their owners and can be given away to a new owner or sold for a fee. But even servant-slaves have rights – and these are strictly guarded by Benin customs and laws. It seems odd to foreign visitors, but servant-slaves in Benin can own property of their own, are allowed time off to work for themselves, and are free to marry and have families of their own. People become servant-slaves by being the children of servant-slaves or by being captured in war. Sometimes they become servant-slaves for a short while as a way to repay their debts.

TIME-TRAVELER'S GUIDE

POWERFUL GODS

People in Benin worship a family of powerful gods. Osanobua is the great Creator God who made the earth and all living things. He created many children for himself, and the people of Benin worship them as gods, too.

Olokun is the most important and popular of Osanobua's sons. He is "lord of the great waters" (the sea, the rivers, and the rain). He loves beauty and brings health, wealth, and many children. He is especially worshiped by women, and most homes have a little shrine to Olokun, where women place offerings of chalk, for purity and good fortune, and fresh water, which they put in a special pot.

Another of Osanobua's powerful sons is Ogiuwu, the terrifying lord of death. He has a shrine in the center of Benin City, where people offer him sacrifices. Ogun is protector of farmers, craftsmen, hunters, and warriors. Osun is an invisible god – the magic power in forest trees and leaves. Obiemwen, one of Osanobua's daughters, protects women in childbirth.

SPIRITS & ANCESTORS

The people of Benin believe that there are two parallel worlds: the invisible world of the spirits and the visible, everyday world, where we all live. They also believe that these two worlds are interconnected. Invisible spirits can make things happen in the everyday world, and people can also call on the invisible power of the spirit world to help them in their daily lives.

Although the mightiest spirits are the gods themselves, people believe that the spirits of their dead ancestors also have great power. When a man dies, his eldest son builds an altar for his spirit in the family home, puts a special staff there, and on festival days makes offerings to him on behalf of the entire family. He asks for advice and blessing from his dead father's spirit, just as he would have while his father was alive. After a while, the dead man's spirit will be reborn in a new baby belonging to the family and so begin a whole new life. Benin people believe that this happens fourteen times before a spirit finally stays in the spirit world.

FESTIVALS

Each village has its own special festivals, but in Benin City itself the festival year begins in March, with Ikhurhe or "Clearing the Land." This is designed to purify the soil and ensure plentiful crops.

The festivals of Eghute and Orhu are designed to bring fertility, to both families and fields, and to drive evil out of Benin City.

The festival year ends with two more important festivals – Erha Oba, which honors the Oba's dead father, and Igue, which is intended to increase the living Oba's magical powers. These festivals are splendid occasions. Everyone wears their best clothes and takes part in the many processions. At Erha Oba, the Oba dances in front of his dead father's altar. At Igue, the Oba is anointed with a magic potion, brewed from forest herbs. On the last day of this festival, children from Benin City go out into the forest and bring home armfuls of "ewere" leaves, which they call "leaves of joy," to bring happiness and hope to their families in the coming year.

GUIDED TOURS

BEFORE YOU START

You'll enjoy exploring the city much more if you can say a few words and phrases in Edo. It will also show the people you meet that you are really interested in them and their city.

If you are greeting a man, say "Do," but remember that it is "Ko" if you are speaking to a woman. "Obowie" is "Good morning" and "Obota" is "Good evening."

If you are lucky enough to meet a chief, an elder, or some other important person, "Domo" is what you must say. It shows that you are respectful and know their importance.

If you visit someone's home, people will say "Obokhian" to you as you are introduced. In reply, you must say "Obowa."

And remember that it is important always to say "Oba gha to kpere, Ise," "Long may the Oba reign," after prayers.

On festival days people will greet you with the phrase "Iselogbe," "Happy celebration." Return their greeting.

THE OBA'S MARKET & THE ROYAL PALACE

The best place to start your tour of the city is at the Ughoton gate. This is one of the main entrances to the city and is the one used by most foreign visitors. It stands at the end of one of the most important routes in the empire – the broad road that runs from Benin City to the port of Ughoton.

Like the other eight city gates, the Ughoton gate is made of tropical hardwood. It is very strong, and there are always soldiers on watch at the gates, keeping an eye on everyone who enters the city.

Before you go through the gate, pause to admire the massive city walls. They have been built up over many years and are now so big that it is difficult to realize that they are made only of layers of mud.

Now go through the gate – and be prepared for a surprise. Many visitors are amazed at just how large and built-up it is. As soon as you enter, you will see the Ekenwan Road, the city's broad main

street, stretching away from you in an impressively straight line as far as the eye can see.

There are another 30 or so major thoroughfares in the city, all linked together by a maze of little courtyards, back-streets, and narrow alleyways. Ordinary people live and work there. As you make your way along the main street, you will pass through many different "quarters" or "wards" of the city, where people skilled at particular crafts and trades all live and work together. (If you want to explore this area, the next tour tells you how.)

As you draw close to the center of the city, the noise of hundreds of people laughing, talking, and bargaining will tell you that you are near the city's main shopping area. Soon you will see it – the Oba's Market – stretching away on your right. This is where many of the goods the craftspeople make are bought and sold – along with all kinds of rare and interesting things from the local countryside and farther afield.

If you have the time, it is worth spending a whole morning in the market, just wandering around and looking.

When you leave the market, walk a little farther

along the Ekenwan Road. There, ahead of you, are the walls of the Oba's palace.

If you have time, go and stand outside the main gateway, to watch the important visitors – chiefs, foreign ambassadors, and army commanders among them – hurrying in and out on their way to meet the Oba or to carry out important business for the empire. They will all be dressed in their best clothes and attended by smart, well-trained servants. Many will also have gifts to offer the Oba.

When you've seen as much as you want to, turn around with your back to the palace. In the distance you will see the Town Chiefs' quarters. Some of the city's richest men live there, in fine houses built around large courtyards. Like other homes in the city, they are single-storied, but they are larger and have walls coated with shiny red clay. Outside they are decorated with patterns and moldings of animals and warriors.

If you are visiting the city on a festival day – and that is the best time to be there – you may hear the sounds of slow, stately music and dancing from the Oba's palace, along with songs praising the Oba. But the sounds sometimes change when the Oba has important visitors. Many of them would bring musicians to provide

entertainment for the Oba.

At this point, after visiting the palace, you may feel that you have walked quite far enough in the strong sunshine. If so, turn around and retrace your steps to the Oba's market-place, buy something to eat and drink, and have a rest. If you don't feel like walking that far, look for one of the many small, local markets. There is bound to be one nearby.

THE CRAFTWORKERS' QUARTERS

Start this tour from outside the Oba's palace. Head eastward along the main street until you hear the noise of hammering and smell the smoke from wood and charcoal fires. These signs will tell you that you have reached the ironworkers' area.

You will see ironsmiths and their assistants hard at work, using bellows to fan the flames inside the baked-clay furnaces until the iron glows red-hot.

When you have seen enough, make your way back to the main street. Cross over, then head north, threading your way through the tangle of

narrow lanes. Keep walking northward, and you will get to the leatherworkers' quarter. But be prepared for a long walk, because their workshops are on the far edge of the built-up area, close to the city walls.

The leatherworkers' area is a real maze, full of smells and flies. There are heaps of animal skins everywhere: fresh ones waiting to be cleaned and tanned, newly treated ones pegged out to dry in the sun, and finished ones neatly stacked and ready for sale.

If you can find your way through the leatherworkers' area, head northeast to a very interesting part of the city – the place where drums and other musical instruments are made.

Slow, stately music and dancing are important at occasions like weddings, funerals, and the crowning of an Oba. Ordinary people also enjoy faster and more exciting music and dancing, and that's what you'll see and hear at any festival you go to.

After the noise, heat, and bustle of your visit to the craft workshops, you will be tired and probably hungry. To get back to the city center by the quickest route, head toward the walls – they're so big that they're a good landmark – and keep on walking beside them until you reach the main street again.

COUNTRYSIDE TOUR

To explore the countryside around the city, you can leave by any gate. The best-known road out of the city is the one that runs between Ughoton and Benin City. You will find that it has "refreshment points" at regular intervals, where officials sell drinking water from big clay pots. If you find one of these refreshment points unattended, don't worry. You can help yourself to a drink (for a cup, use one of the big shells provided) and leave your pay-ment; no one will steal it.

The Ughoton road is clearly marked and well used. If you plan to explore the country-side far beyond the city, it is best to stick to such well-trodden routes. The thick, dense rain forest is wonderful to look at but very easy for visitors to get lost in once they leave the beaten track. In fact, you would be wise to hire a knowledgeable local guide. Then you can enjoy exploring the countryside with-out having to worry about how you'll get back!

Magnificent trees are a feature of Benin's countryside.

Almost everywhere you travel, you will be surrounded by the tropical rain forest. Look out for stately iroko trees (which local people believe to be sacred), magnificent mahogany and ebony trees, kola nut trees, and oil-palms.

The trees and plants of the rain forest provide the people of Benin with many useful things, including building materials, food, and fuel. The bark, roots, and seeds of the plants also give ingredients for medicines. But don't eat any of the plants or fruit unless you know exactly what they are — there are many poisonous plants in the forest.

The rain forest is also a wonderful place for wildlife. It is home to a large number of wild creatures – such as monkeys, antelopes, bush-rats, and red wart-hogs. There are scorpions, huge spiders, and poisonous snakes, including black cobras, as well as pythons that wrap themselves around their prey and crush it to death. You might be lucky enough to see a majestic vulturine fish eagle or a brilliantly colored parrot swooping among the trees.

The rain forest is so interesting that you'll want to look around you all the time as you walk, but do take care where you put your feet — there

are many thick, twining vines that will trip up the unwary. Other hazards to avoid are getting your leg trapped in a hunter's snare or falling into a wart-hog pit-trap dug by men from a nearby village.

If you want to go hunting, you should consult an expert. Elephant hunters live in the village of Oregbeni (which means "the place where they kill elephants"), just outside Benin City. Specialist leopard-hunters, who work for the Oba, live in Benin City itself. Safer game to hunt are tortoises and fist-sized snails, which taste good when they are cooked.

The mighty River Niger forms the eastern boundary of the kingdom of Benin, and the Ethiope River flows through the southernmost parts of the land. If you dare, you might want to take a river trip in a dugout canoe — but beware of the crocodiles and poisonous snakes that live in all the rivers.

If you get to the north-western borders of the empire, close to the town of Otun, you will see rows of huge trees towering above the low-growing bush. Tradition records that the trees were planted by soldiers from Benin and its rival king-dom, Oyo, to mark the frontier between their kingdoms, which were often at war.

VISITING VILLAGES & FARMS

Benin is a large and splendid city, but many of the Oba's subjects do not live there. Instead they live in villages and work on farms. They produce most of the food that is sold in the city and raw materials, like cotton and skins, for city craft-workers to use.

To visit a village you must first contact the chief appointed by the Oba to supervise the village. The chief is often a relative of the Oba. Then you must contact the village's head-man, who is always the oldest man. He and the elders supervise community activities, perform religious rituals, and ensure that the law is upheld.

The headman will explain that village people usually live in large, extended families. Grandparents, parents, aunts, uncles, children, and grand-children all live in one big compound, with separate rooms for different family members.

You will also discover that for village men, community life is organized into three different age-groups – youths, adults, and elders. Members of each age-

group work together at community tasks, such as clearing paths (youths), fighting invaders (adults), and settling disputes (elders). Women of all ages will tell you that they too work hard, caring for their husbands and children, raising animals, and growing food for their family.

As you explore, you will see that patches of rain forest have been cut down to make room for fields and farms. If you are visiting Benin during February or March, you may see this forest clearing in progress. First, the men clear the under-growth with their machetes. The plants are left for several days to dry in the hot sun, before being burned. Some of the smaller trees are cut down as well, with iron-bladed axes. The trunks and branches are neatly trimmed and saved for later use, to support climbing plants like pepper-vines. The largest trees are too difficult to fell, so they are left standing in the cleared area.

If you arrive in the countryside during April, you will see whole families busy planting yams in the fields that were cleared earlier that year. First, they make rows of little mounds in the soil, using hand-held hoes. Next, they plant a seed-yam in each little

mound. (A seed-yam is a particularly healthy yam tuber that has been stored by the farmer since the last harvest. By April, it is beginning to send out shoots. The farmer cuts sections of the tuber, each with a nice fresh shoot, and buries each section in the soil, where it grows into a new plant.)

Everyone helps gather the yams in the dry season. Then they celebrate, with music, dancing, and people dressed as gods and legendary figures going through the streets.

As you travel through Benin's farmland, you will see that some farm plots look abandoned or are covered with rough, scrubby plants. This is because the soil will only grow good crops for a few seasons. Then the farmers leave the plot to become forest again for up to twenty years, after which it will be ready to grow crops again. Look out for crossed sticks by the side of the road. It means a family has earmarked the plot for cultivation later in the year.

You may sometimes see fields planted with crops in isolated forest clearings, far from any village. Crop failure can mean starvation and death, so most families try to cultivate at least two farms. Then, if the crops fail at one farm, they may not at the other.

GLOSSARY

Agate Semiprecious stone, often a reddish-brown color.

Ancestors People we are descended from, who lived long ago.

Anklets Bracelets worn round the ankles.

Barter To "buy" and "sell" goods by exchanging them for items of a similar value.

Bast Stringy plant fiber, used to weave baskets, mats, and cloth.

Brass Shiny reddish-yellow metal, made from a mixture of copper and zinc.

Bronze Shiny reddish-yellow metal, made from a mixture of copper and tin.

Coral Precious material formed from the skeletons of tiny sea creatures.

Cowrie Shellfish that live in tropical waters. Cowrie shells were used as a form of money in Benin.

Earthworks Huge mounds or walls made of earth.

Empire Large area of land, often including several different peoples, governed by the ruler of the strongest nation.

Extended family Large group of relatives living together, including several generations: grandparents, parents, children, in-laws, cousins, uncles, and aunts.

Guild Groups of craftworkers who maintain high standards and organize the training of young workers.

Iroko Tall tropical tree, valued for its beautiful, very hard wood.

Kola nuts Nuts from a tropical tree. They have a stimulating effect like caffeine.

Machetes Sharp, wide-bladed knives.

Manillas Heavy copper bracelets, brought to Benin by Portuguese traders to exchange for Benin goods.

Molten Melted.

Mudfish Large fish that live in the rivers of Benin.

Oba Benin's ruler, or king.

Okra Plant that grows in warm countries. Its small green pods are used as a vegetable.

Palace Chiefs Members of ancient noble families. They run the Oba's palace, supervize royal ceremonies, and act as advisers to the royal family.

Papaya South American fruit tree brought to Africa by the Portuguese. The fruit is sweet and good to eat.

Plaque Slab or plate with writing or carving on it, usually fixed to a wall.

Prophecy Foretelling the future or passing on a religious message.

Raffia Plant fiber, used to weave baskets, mats, and cloth.

Shrine Holy place, where people say prayers and make offerings.

Terra-cotta Clay fired at a fairly low temperature to produce reddish-brown pottery.

Town Chiefs Leaders chosen from rich ordinary families. They keep law and order, act as local governors, and collect taxes.

Yam Starchy plant tubers cooked and eaten as food.

INDEX